Four Bath Buns

Written by Amanda Overeynder and illustrated by Susie Grindey

ISBN 978-190305-636-5

Published under licence by Brown Dog Books and The Self Publishing Partnership
7 Green Park Station, Bath BA1 1JB
www.selfpublishingpartnership.co.uk

Printed and bound by Butler Tanner & Dennis, Frome, Somerset BA11 1NF

Four Bath Buns

These are not just ordinary buns, these are the Four Bath Buns!

This is Bonne Bonne Bun, the grandmother, the original Bath Bun! She was born in Bath in the house next door to The Theatre Royal. Beau Nash, the man who made Bath famous in the 18th century, had also lived in the house.

Bonne Bonne adores beautiful Bath and she loves cooking. Her daughter Jayne and her grandchildren, Rosie and Flo, the little Bath Buns, love cooking too.

When Jayne was a little girl, Bonne Bonne used to take her to Hands' Dairy near The Roman Baths, for scones with jam and cream and a strawberry milkshake. In the dairy Bonne Bonne would buy thick cream which Mrs Hands would ladle out of a big earthenware bowl on the counter. It was so delicious spread on scones, with Victoria plum jam.

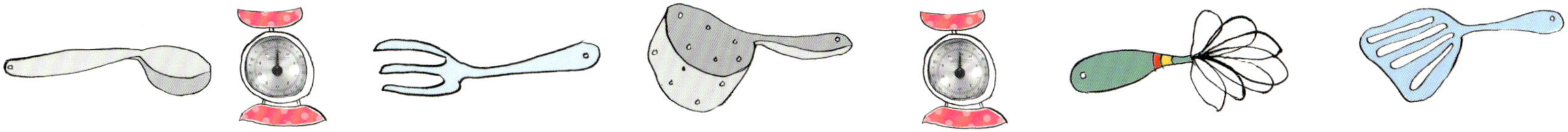

Scrumptious Scones

(makes about 10)
250gm (10 oz) self raising-flour
50gm (2oz) butter/margarine
25gm (1 oz) caster sugar
300ml (1/2 pint) natural yoghurt
1 heaped teaspoon baking powder

Heat the oven to 180ºC/gas mark 5.
Place the flour in a large bowl with the baking powder.
Rub in the butter/margarine with your fingertips.
Add the sugar and stir through.
Add the yoghurt and stir/mix to a soft dough, adding a little milk if needed.
Form a ball of dough and turn out on to a well-floured surface.
Pat out to 3cm thick and cut out circles using a floured 8cm cutter.
Place on a baking sheet and bake in the oven for 12-15mins until golden brown.
Cool on a wire rack.
Enjoy with jam and cream ... yummy!

Rosie and Flo often go to stay with Bonne Bonne for the weekend. They love to pull on their wellies and paddle in the brook which runs near the house and to pick blackberries and apples from the orchard.

Fruit crumble with custard is always a favourite with Flo when they get back home.

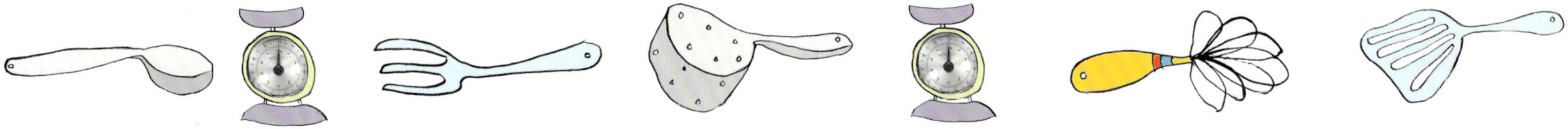

Blackberry and Apple Crumble

3 large Bramley cooking apples
150gm (6oz) blackberries
(raspberries or blackcurrants
are also very good!)
50gm (2oz) granulated sugar

Crumble mixture
200gm (8oz) self raising flour
100gm (4oz) butter/margarine
50gm (2oz) vanilla caster sugar

Peel and slice the apples into a large saucepan.
Add the blackberries and sugar and 2 tablespoons of water.
Gently stew for 10 mins, until the apple has softened.
Tip into a flat crumble dish.

Heat the oven to 180°C.
Put the flour into a large bowl.
Cut the butter/margarine into small cubes and add to the flour.
Rub the fat into the flour using your fingertips, until there are no lumps!
Stir in the caster sugar.

Top the stewed fruit with the crumble mixture.
Cook in the oven for 20 minutes, until golden, then sprinkle with
a little caster sugar.

Rosie and Flo can't decide if ice cream or custard is best with crumble.
They sometimes have both!

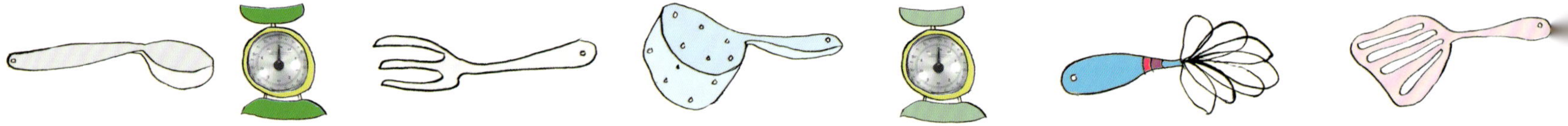

Syrupy Baked Apples

6 large dessert apples
50gm (2oz) desiccated coconut
50gm (2oz) sultanas
25gm (1oz) soft brown sugar
50gm (2oz) marzipan, finely chopped (optional, but very yummy!)
25gm (1oz) softened butter
2 teaspoons vanilla extract

Preheat oven to 180°C (gas mark 4).
Carefully core each apple using an apple corer.
Cut a thin line in the skin around the circumference of each fruit, to let it expand as it cooks.
Mix together the other ingredients in a bowl.
Place the cored apples in an ovenproof dish.
Carefully fill each apple with the mixture and put any extra filling mixture around the apples in the dish.
Place in the oven and bake for 25-30 minutes.

Serve each apple in a pretty bowl with the syrupy juices spooned over and a scoop of vanilla ice cream.

One day when they were out for a walk Flo asked, 'What's that white flower up there called?' 'That's elderflower,' Bonne Bonne replied. 'Mummy uses elderflower to make elderflower cordial,' said Rosie. 'It's so delicious and refreshing after we've been playing tennis or cricket, especially with a yummy cookie! '

Elderflower Cordial (makes about 500ml)

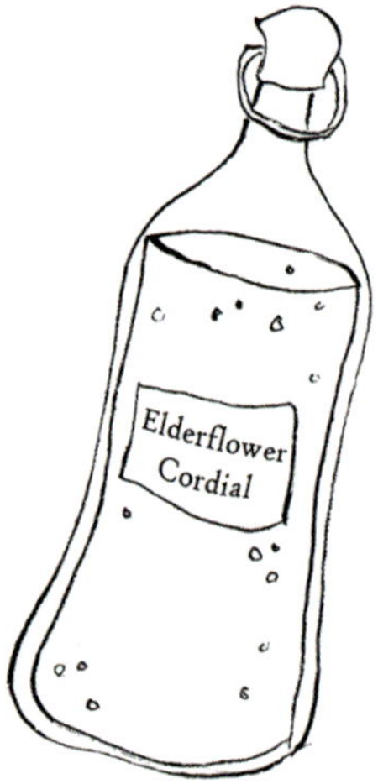

10 fresh elderflower heads
zest and juice of 1 large unwaxed lemon
350gm (14oz) granulated sugar
1 teaspoon citric acid (optional)
400ml (about a pint) boiling water

Place the elderflower heads and lemon zest in a large bowl (watch out for any creepy crawlies!).
Pour over the boiling water and allow to soak for at least 2 hours.
Strain the elderflower water into a large pan through a clean muslin or new kitchen cloth.
Add the sugar and lemon juice to the pan and heat gently to dissolve.
Add the citric acid, if using.
Allow to cool slightly before pouring into very clean glass bottles.
Add a pretty label to the bottle.
Store in the fridge, for up to 4 weeks.
Dilute with still or sparkling water and serve with lots of ice cubes.

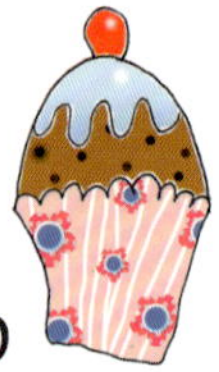

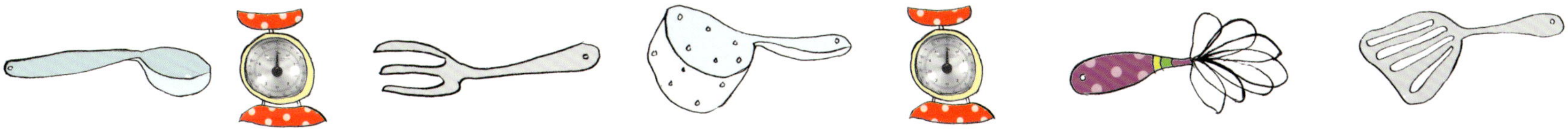

Chocolate Chip and Peanut Butter Cookies (makes about 15)

100gm (4oz) butter (softened)
75gm (3oz) soft brown sugar
75gm (3oz) caster sugar
1 egg (beaten)
1 large tablespoon peanut butter
175gm (6oz) plain flour
1 teaspoon baking powder
150gm (6oz) milk chocolate (chopped)

Preheat the oven to 180°C (gas mark 4).
Cream together the sugars and butter until soft and fluffy.
Add the egg and peanut butter and mix together.
Next add the flour and baking powder and stir together.
Finally mix in the chocolate chunks.
Place spoonfuls of mixture onto a greased baking tray, leaving lots of space for each cookie to spread (about 5 cookies to each tray).
Bake for 14 minutes then take them out of the oven to cool slightly, patting gently with a spatula.
Transfer the cookies to a cooling rack to cool completely.

Rosie and Flo love to eat these warm with a glass of cold milk.

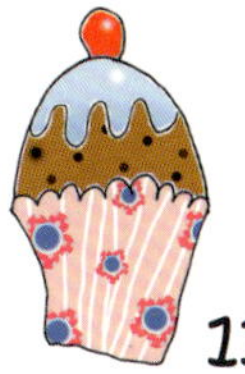

Sometimes Rosie and Bonne Bonne go for a special treat to The Pump Rooms in Bath. It is so magical there with the crystal chandelier twinkling and people sipping the famous Bath water, as they look through the window into the Roman Baths. There are often three musicians who sit on the stage at one end of the room and entertain everyone on piano, violin and cello. It is a real treat! 'What shall we have?' Bonne Bonne asks Rosie. 'I would love a Bath Bun and a strawberry smoothie please,' replies Rosie. Bonne Bonne can't decide whether to try a chocolate brownie or a slice of lemon drizzle cake with her cup of tea! Bath buns are always Rosie's favourite.

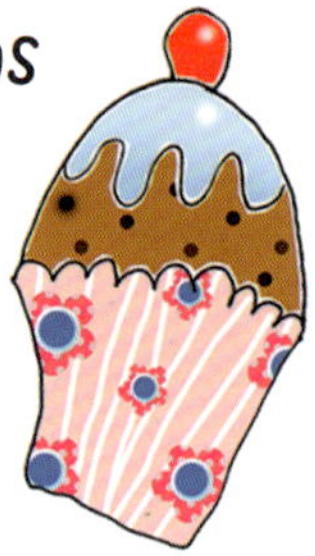

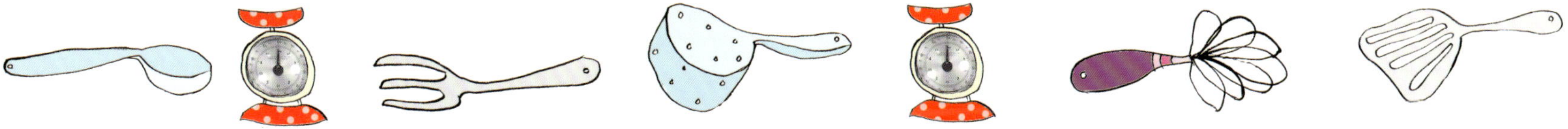

Bath Buns

450gm (16 oz) strong flour
1 sachet dried yeast
50gm (2oz) caster sugar
50gm (2oz) melted butter
2 beaten eggs
150ml warm milk
175gm (6 oz) sultanas/currants
grated zest of 1 lemon & orange
10 sugar lumps!
1 beaten egg and sugar nibbs
(crushed sugar cubes!) to glaze
large lightly greased tray

Put the flour, yeast, caster sugar, lemon and orange zest and sultanas, into a large mixing bowl, or the bowl of a food mixer.
Add the melted butter, beaten eggs and warm milk.
Mix to a soft dough, using the dough hook or a wooden spoon.
Knead for 5 minutes, then cover and leave to rise for 45 minutes, or doubled in size.

If using a food mixer, knead again then tip out the dough onto a floured surface, otherwise tip out the dough and knead.
Divide into 10 equal pieces and shape each piece into a bun, placing a sugar lump in the middle before placing on the greased baking tray.
Leave for 45 minutes, to double in size.
Heat the oven to 190°C.
Brush each bun with beaten egg and sprinkle with the sugar nibbs (that's what makes them a Bath bun!).
Bake in the oven for 15-20 minutes, until golden brown and hollow when tapped on the base.
Cool on a wire rack.

Serve buttered, listening to a string quartet. You could almost be in the Pump Rooms!

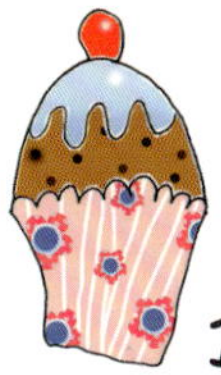

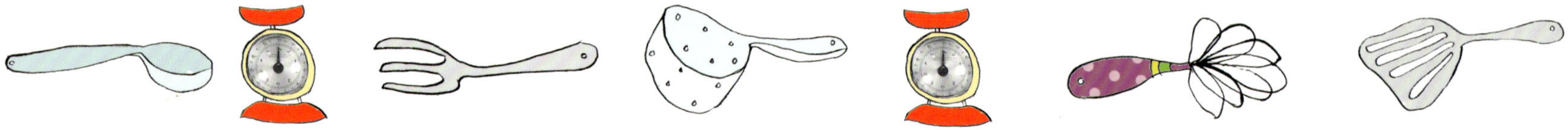

Strawberry Smoothie (makes 2 large glasses)

large handful/punnet of strawberries, about 15 (washed)
one small ripe banana (peeled and chopped)
2 scoops of vanilla ice cream
125ml (1 small pot) natural yogurt
200ml (1/3 pint) milk

Put all the ingredients in a plastic jug and 'blitz' with a hand blender until smooth.
Pour into two large pretty glasses and serve with a straw – very chilled!
Rosie and Flo also love smoothies made with tinned mango and raspberries!

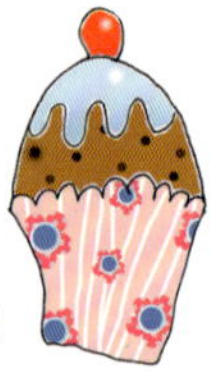

They sit there enjoying their drinks and eating real Bath Buns, which always have a sugar lump in the centre and sugar nibbs on top.

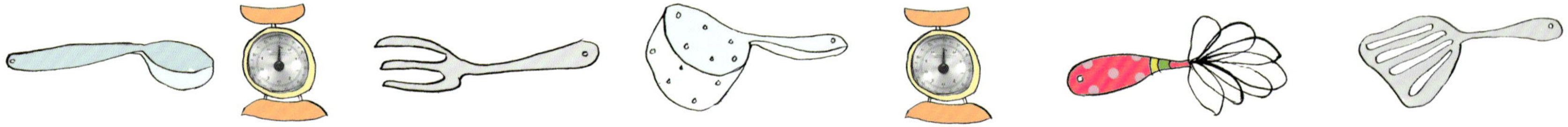

Bonne Bonne's Brownies (makes 18)

100gm (4oz) plain chocolate
150gm (6oz) butter
125gm (5oz) plain flour
15gm (1/2oz) cocoa
half a teaspoon baking powder
1 teaspoon vanilla extract
300gm (12oz) soft brown sugar
2 eggs (beaten)
50gm (2oz) chopped nuts
(walnut, pecan or hazelnut)

Preheat oven to 180°C/gas mark 4.
Grease and line the base of a 20cm x 15cm baking tin with greaseproof pape
Break the chocolate into chunks and place in a large bowl with the butter.
Heat the bowl in the microwave for 15 seconds at a time, until the butter and chocolate are melted.
Mix the chocolate and butter together and leave to cool slightly.
Add all the other ingredients into the bowl with the chocolate mixture.
Stir gently to combine.
Spoon into the prepared tin.
Bake for 25 minutes until the top is set.
Cool in the tin before cutting into squares.

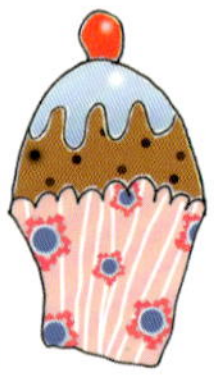

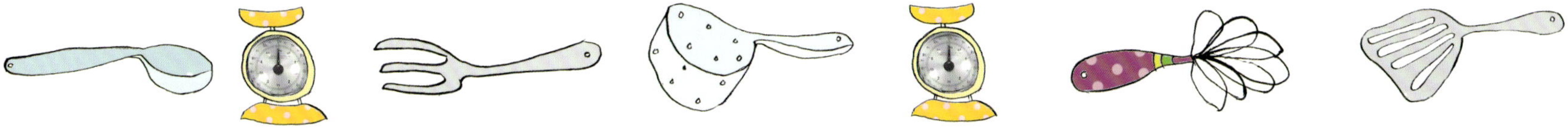

Lemon Drizzle Cake

250gm (10oz) self raising-flour
200gm (8oz) softened butter or margarine
200gm (8oz) caster sugar
half a teaspoon baking powder
3 eggs (beaten)
grated zest of 2 lemons
juice of 2 lemons
100gm (4oz) icing sugar

Preheat the oven to 180ºC/gas mark 4.
Lightly grease and line the base and sides of a loaf tin with greaseproof paper.
Beat together the sugar, butter or margarine and eggs.
Stir in the flour and baking powder.
Add half the lemon zest and half the lemon juice and mix together.
Spoon into the prepared tin.
Bake in the oven for 40 minutes, until golden brown and well risen.
Remove from the oven and leave in the tin.
Use a fork to make a series of holes in the surface of the hot cake.

Mix the icing sugar with the remaining lemon zest and juice.
Pour the icing over the surface of the cake while the cake is still warm and leave to cool completely.
Carefully remove the cake from the tin.

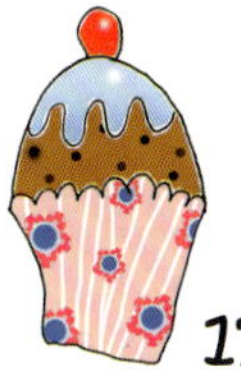

One of the joys of living in Bath is watching the hot air balloons. They frequently 'take off' from the top common in the Royal Victoria Park. Rosie and Flo often go there for a picnic with their parents in the early evening, to watch the balloons prepare and the passengers climb excitedly into the basket under the hot air balloon. The big balloons are so colourful. Red, yellow, purple stripes, orange and green. They rise straight up from the grass into the air as the roar of the burners fills the balloon with hot air. They look wonderful against the blue sky, with the elegant Georgian houses of the Royal Crescent in the background.

Rosie and Flo sit on the grass on their tartan rug and gaze up at the colourful scene as they munch their homemade bread roll twists and hummus.

The girls wonder what other exciting tasty treats Mummy has packed in the picnic basket.

Bread Roll Twists (makes 12)

750gm (1 1/2 lb) strong flour
1 sachet dried yeast (7gm)
2 tablespoons olive oil
500ml (18fl oz) warm water
1 teaspoon salt
1 beaten egg
poppy/sesame seeds

Put flour, yeast, salt and oil in a large bowl (or food mixer with dough hook).
Gradually add warm water and mix to a stiff dough.
Knead in the mixer or by hand for 5 minutes.
Leave the bowl, covered with a tea towel, in a warm place to 'prove' – that means double in size!
Tip the dough out onto a floured surface. Shape into a round and divide into 12 evenly sized pieces.
Roll each piece into a long sausage shape and tie a simple loop knot!
Place on a lightly greased baking sheet, brush with beaten egg and sprinkle with poppy/sesame seeds.
Leave to rise for 20 minutes. Turn on oven to 200°C/gas mark 6 to pre-heat.
Bake in the hot oven for 15-20 minutes until golden brown and hollow-sounding when tapped.
Cool on a wire rack.

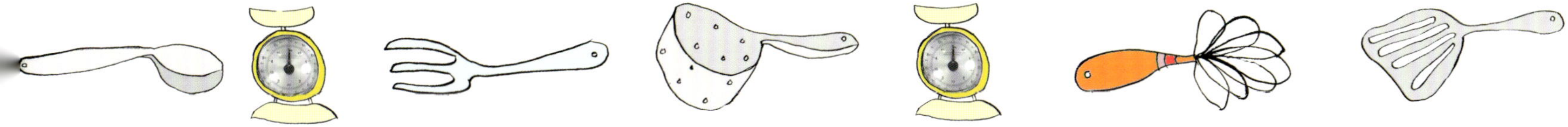

Hummus

1 tin (410 gm) of chickpeas – drained
1 clove of garlic
1 tablespoon tahini (sesame paste)
4 tablespoons olive oil
juice of one lemon
pinch of salt and twist of black pepper
1-2 tablespoons of boiling water (if required)

Put all the ingredients in a large bowl or blender jug.
Blitz with a hand-held food blender or in a food processor (adult help required!!).
Add a little boiling water to get a soft smooth consistency.
Serve in a bowl drizzled with a little olive oil and balsamic vinegar.

Enjoy with bread roll twists, warmed pitta bread, or raw vegetable sticks ... delicious!

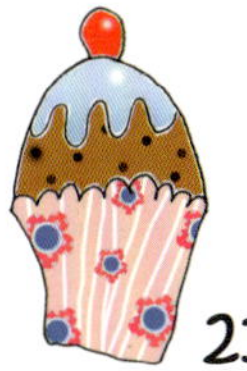

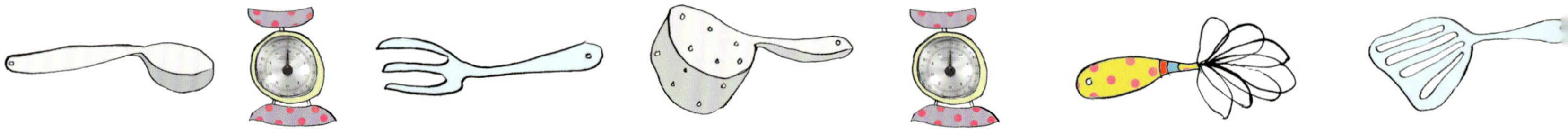

Tasty Cheese Straws (makes about 20)

100gm (4oz) self raising-flour
50gm (2oz) butter (chopped)
100gm (4oz) finely grated strong tasty cheddar cheese
1 teaspoon Dijon mustard
twist of pepper
1 egg yolk
2 teaspoons cold water

Heat oven to 180ºC/gas mark 4.
Put flour in large bowl with butter.
Rub butter into flour until it looks like fine breadcrumbs.
Stir in grated cheese, mustard powder and pepper.
Bind together into a ball with beaten egg yolk and teaspoons of cold water, if needed.
Roll out 'pastry' on a lightly floured surface to 1cm thick.
Cut into thin 'straws' about half a cm wide.
Place on a baking sheet.
Cook for 8-10 minutes in preheated oven, until golden brown.
Cool on a cooling rack.

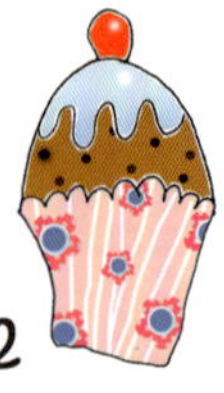

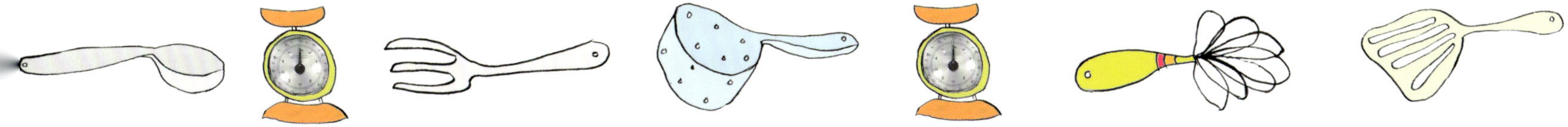

Picnic Sausage Rolls (makes 12 - 14)

500gm (1lb 2oz) sausage meat or skinned sausages
I packet of shortcrust or puff pastry approx. 500gm
1 small red onion, finely chopped
1 beaten egg – to glaze

Preheat oven to 180°C/gas mark 4.
On a lightly floured surface, roll out the pastry thinly to make a square, about 30cm wide.
In a bowl, mix together the sausage meat and the chopped red onion.
Cut the square of pastry down the middle to make two rectangles.
Divide the sausage meat mixture into two halves.
Make each half into a sausage shape and place down the long side of one piece of the pastry.
Brush the edge with beaten egg and flap over the pastry to cover the sausage meat.
Press the edges together and use a fork to make a pattern along the sealed edges.
Cut into 6 - 8 equal-sized pieces and place on a baking sheet.
Glaze each sausage roll with the beaten egg.
Repeat with the other half of the mixture and pastry.
Bake in the preheated oven for 25 minutes until golden brown.
Cool on a wire rack.

Enjoy with some homemade chutney.

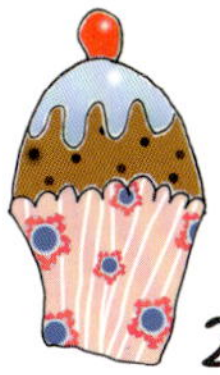

When the weather turns cold, Rosie and Flo still love to have fun outdoors. On Bonfire Night in November they go to the recreation ground in the centre of Bath (where the Bath rugby team play!) and watch the fireworks.

The River Avon flows alongside the recreation ground and they sit on the river bank on a warm blanket where they can see the floodlit Abbey, Pulteney Bridge and the amazing fireworks. Jayne knows it will be chilly so she puts some of their favourite leek and potato soup into a big flask, and packs some apricot flapjacks too.

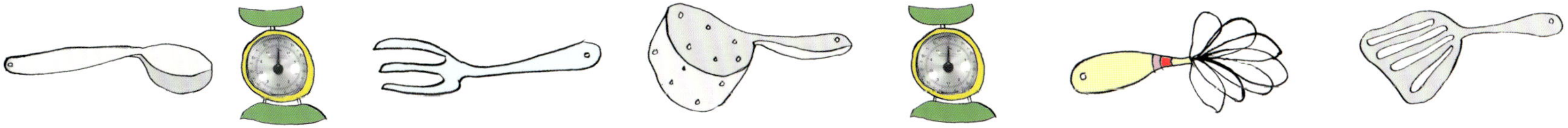

Leek and Potato Soup (serves 4)

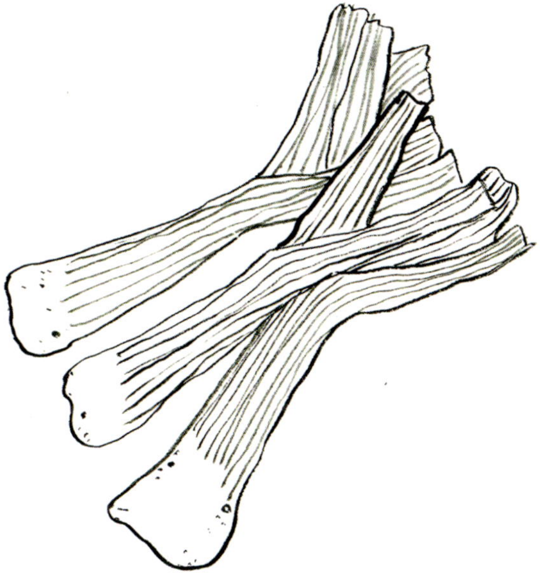

3 leeks
1 large/2 medium potatoes
1 onion
1 glove of garlic
1 tablespoon oil
25gm (1oz) butter
1 litre (2 pints) chicken/vegetable stock

Chop and wash the leeks (white and green parts).
Peel and chop the potatoes into small chunks.
Peel and chop the onion and garlic.
Heat the oil and butter in a large saucepan.
Gently fry the onion for a few minutes, then add the leeks and garlic and fry for a further 5 minutes.
Add the potato chunks and stir together for a few minutes.
Add the stock to cover the vegetables and simmer (boil very gently) for 15 minutes, until the potatoes are cooked.
Turn off the heat and allow the soup to cool slightly before blitzing to a smooth puree with a hand-held blender.
Season to taste with a little pepper and salt.

You can add chopped parsley and a swirl of cream for a snazzy finish!

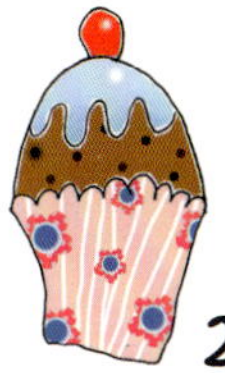

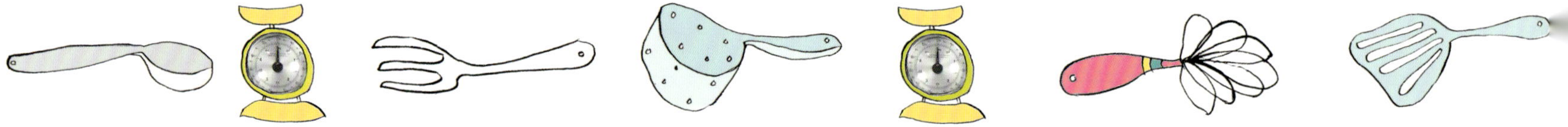

Apricot Flapjacks (makes 16)

225gm (8oz) margarine
225gm (8oz) demerara sugar
2 tablespoons golden syrup
275gm (10oz) rolled oats
100gm (4oz) chopped apricots

Heat the oven to 160°C/gas mark 3.
Lightly grease a 20cm square baking tin.
Gently heat the margarine in a saucepan.
Add the golden syrup (heat the spoon up first in a mug of hot water) and sugar and heat gently until they dissolve.
Turn off the heat and add the oats and chopped apricots.
Stir carefully until the oats are mixed with the buttery sugary syrup.
Tip the mixture into the greased baking tin and flatten down.
Cook in the preheated oven until golden brown (30 minutes).
Leave to cool for a while in the tin on a cooling rack.
Cut into 16 small squares and leave to cool completely in the tin.

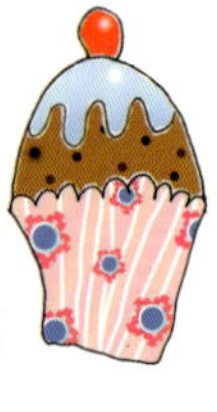

Both Rosie and Flo have their birthdays in November. They love to do something a little different each year and always plan their activities well in advance. Last year they planned a bicycle ride with their friends along the Kennet and Avon Canal from Limpley Stoke to Avoncliffe. 'Bonne Bonne, please will you meet us when we arrive, in your camper van, and bring "pasta meaties" for us to have?' asked Rosie. 'Always pleased to oblige,' Bonne Bonne laughed. It was a dry day and all the children met Jayne, with their bikes, in the car park at the boating station near Bath.

They set off on their birthday cycle ride. Although it was quite chilly, there was sunshine and the cycling kept them warm. They saw many ducks and swans on their journey and eventually arrived at Avoncliffe near the aqueduct.

Bonne Bonne had made 'pasta meaties' from Jayne's recipe and took it in a large pan with eight plates so the girls could 'tuck in' when they arrived. Bonne Bonne also brought the girls some of their favourite raspberry muffins as a treat.

As Bonne Bonne waited in the camper van she was quite relieved to see a group of giggling girls she recognized riding along on the other side of the canal, and they all cheered when they spotted her. 'Hi, Bonne Bonne,' shouted Rosie and Flo, too nervous to wave and take one hand off the handle bars in case they wobbled. 'We'll ride over the bridge and be with you soon.'

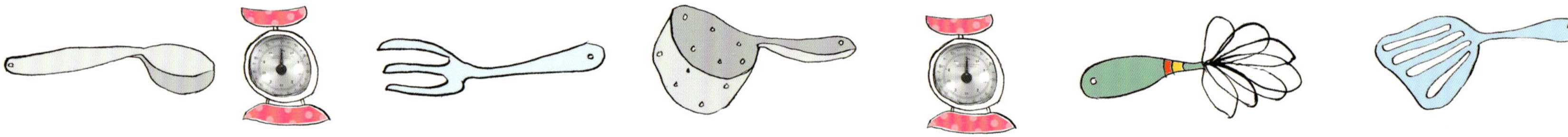

Pasta Meaties (bolognaise-type sauce) – enough for four

200gm (8oz) minced beef
2 rashers smoked bacon (chopped)
1 onion (chopped)
1 glove of garlic (crushed)
1 box/jar (500ml) tomato pasata (puree)
1 tablespoon of olive oil

In a large pan heat the olive oil and add the chopped onion.
Fry gently for 3 or 4 minutes.
Add the chopped bacon to the pan and stir occasionally until cooked.
Add the crushed garlic and the minced beef and continue to fry gently until the meat is cooked.
Add the pasata and stir to mix and heat through.

Cook your favourite pasta to serve with your 'meaties'.

This is delicious served with grated cheese, some homemade pesto and a mixed green salad.

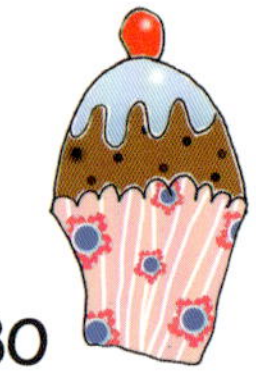

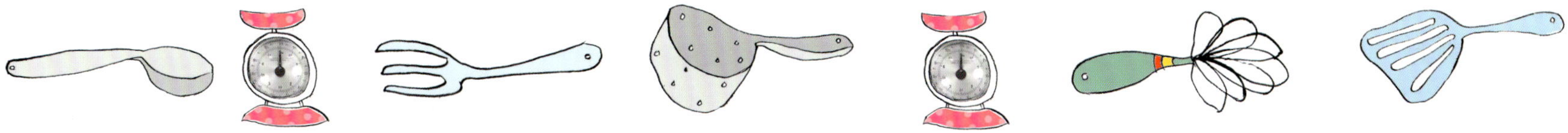

Raspberry and White Chocolate Muffins (makes 12 muffins)

1 egg (beaten)
2 tablespoons sunflower oil
275ml (1/2 pint) milk
300gm (9oz) self raising-flour
2 teaspoons baking powder
100gm (4oz) granulated sugar
125gm (5oz) fresh/frozen raspberries
125gm (5oz) white chocolate (chopped)

Preheat the oven to 200°C/gas mark 6.
Mix the egg, milk and oil together in a jug.
Sieve the flour and baking powder into a large bowl.
Stir in the sugar.
Fold the egg mixture into the flour mixture until all the flour has been mixed (try not to over-mix at this stage).
Gently stir in the raspberries and chocolate.
Put the muffin cases into a muffin tray and carefully spoon in the mixture.
Bake in the oven for 25 minutes until golden and well risen.
Cool on a baking rack and sprinkle with a little caster sugar.

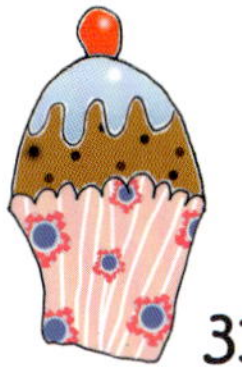

The 'pasta meaties' were a big success and they chatted excitedly about the noisy ducks they had seen, and the two scottie dogs, one black and one white, who were out for a walk. They all remembered seeing the beautiful long boat and had waved to the people on board.

Having been 'fed and watered' the children set off again on their bicycles for their homeward journey and more fun and games at home, with some scrumptious chocolate and raspberry cake.

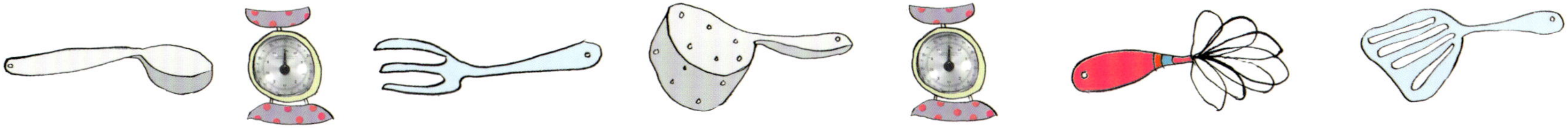

Chocolate and Raspberry Cake

200gm (8oz) caster sugar
200gm (8oz) soft margarine
4 eggs
200gm (8oz) self-raising flour
1 teaspoon baking powder
50gm (2oz) cocoa powder
125gm (5oz) bar of chocolate, chopped into chunks
(milk, plain or white, or a mixture!)
large handful of raspberries

Heat oven to 180°C/gas mark 6.
Grease and line a 20cm square baking tin.
Cream together margarine and sugar.
Add beaten eggs, flour, baking powder and cocoa and beat to form a smooth batter, adding a little milk if very stiff.
Gently stir through the raspberries. Tip into prepared tin and smooth the surface.
Randomly push the chocolate chunks into the surface of the batter; they will gradually drop into the cake as it cooks.
Bake in the oven for 25-30 minutes, until the surface gently springs back when touched (that's a job for an adult!).
Cool on a wire rack.
Dust with icing sugar, and a little drizzled melted chocolate, if you like.
Can be served warm with ice cream for a dessert ... very scrummy!

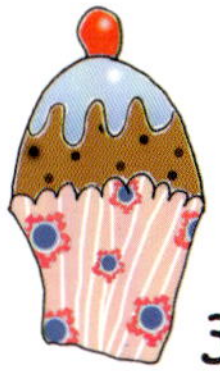

At Christmas time Rosie and Flo sing at their school carol service in Bath Abbey.

It is so exciting to be in the centre of Bath at this time of year, when i is already dark by late afternoon and the lights on the tall Christmas tree in the Abbey Churchyard twinkle and the Nativity manger scer is illuminated.

'Let's go to our special shop in Margaret's Buildings,' suggests Flo. 'Oh yes,' agrees Rosie, 'then we can look at the Christmas market stalls on the way.' They set off on their way through the streets brightly festooned with Christmas lights, chatting about which decoration they are going to buy to go on the Christmas tree. When they reach The Circus, they look up at the acorns which John Wood, the 18th-century architect, had designed to go at the top of the buildings there, and then they walk along Brock Street, which joins The Royal Crescent to The Circus.

Soon they reach their destination and the children excitedly peer in through the window at all the sparkling baubles and jewels.

They tiptoe through the door and look with delight at all the stars, angels, doves, snowflakes and trinkets. At last Rosie chooses a beautiful angel carved from wood and Flo picks a cheerful shepherd to add to their Christmas tree decorations.

After a special hot chocolate with whipped cream, a slice of apple and cinnamon cake and a shortbread biscuit in the nearby cafe, the girls have another look at all the fascinating things in the shop windows. Rosie and Flo are reluctant to leave the magical charm of the quaint shopping street, but Jayne promises them that when they get home they can make Christmas star biscuits to hang on the tree.

Jayne has been making these herself since she was a young girl. The additional promise of breakfast pancakes ensures that the start of the Christmas holiday is full of fun and excitement.

Christmas Star Biscuits (makes about 20)

50gm (2oz) caster sugar
100gm (4oz) butter (softened)
125gm (5oz) plain flour
25gm (1oz) cornflour

Heat oven to 170°C/gas mark 3
In a large bowl cream together the butter and sugar.
Gradually add the plain flour and cornflour and keep mixing until a ball of dough is formed – you may need to use your hands at the end!
Turn onto a floured surface and roll out carefully to about half a centimetre.
Using a floured star cutter, cut out star shapes and place on a baking sheet.
Reform any extra dough, roll and cut out more stars until all the dough has been used up.
To hang on the Christmas tree, make a small round hole at the top of each biscuit before baking.
Thread with pretty ribbons when cool.
Bake in the oven for 12 to 15 minutes, until golden.
Cool on wire rack, dusting with a little caster sugar whilst still warm.
These biscuits can be iced with a simple icing sugar and water icing, and decorated with gold and silver edible baubles ... very festive!

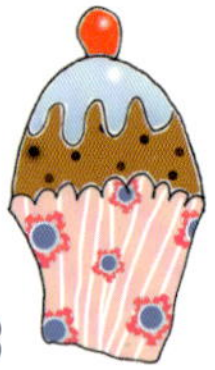

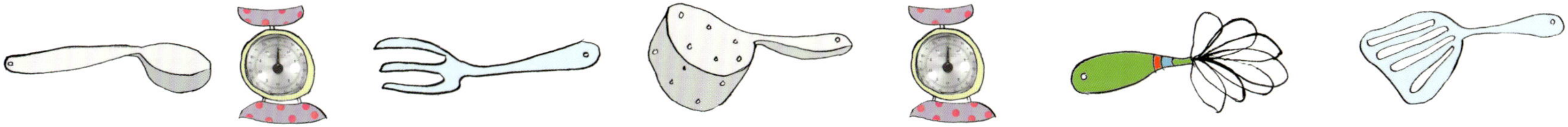

Apple and Cinnamon Cake

200gm (8oz) self raising-flour
200gm (8oz) caster sugar
200gm (8oz) butter or margarine
3 eggs
1 teaspoons baking powder
1 tablespoon boiling water (ask an adult to help with that)
1 large cooking apple, peeled and sliced
100gm (8oz) sultanas
1 teaspoon cinnamon
25gm (1oz) demerara sugar to sprinkle

Preheat the oven to 170°C/gas mark 4.
Lightly grease and line the base of a 23cm round cake tin.
Put the flour, sugar, butter or margarine, baking powder, cinnamon and eggs into a large bowl.
Mix together for about 2 minutes.
Add the boiling water to loosen the mix.
Add the sliced apple and sultanas to the cake mixture and stir together.
Spoon the mixture into the cake tin and level with a spoon.
Sprinkle with the demerara sugar.
Bake in the oven for about 50 minutes until well risen and golden brown.
Cool in the tin for 5 minutes, then loosen and turn out onto a cooling rack.
Dust with icing sugar before serving.

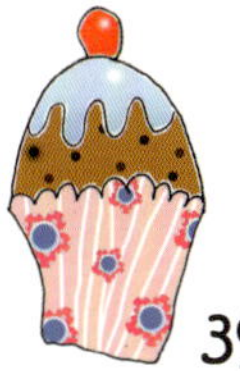

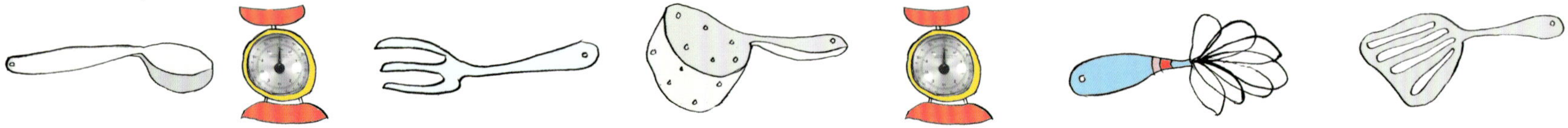

Breakfast Pancakes (makes about 8/10)

8 tablespoons (225gm) (8oz) plain flour
2 eggs
1pint (570ml) of milk
25gm (1oz) butter/margarine for cooking

Put flour into a large bowl.
Crack eggs carefully into the centre of the flour.
Use a balloon whisk and start to mix the flour and eggs together.
Gradually add the milk and continue to mix.
Beat well until you have a smooth batter.

Heat a pancake pan (or frying pan) with a small amount of butter or margarine.
Spoon a ladle of batter into the pan, and swirl to reach the edge of the pan, and leave to cook for about 2 minutes.
'Flip' or turn the pancake carefully, using a palette knife, and cook the other side, until golden and crispy at the edges.

Enjoy these warm pancakes with your favourite toppings! Rosie and Flo love lemon, whipped cream, chocolate sprinkles, strawberries and icing sugar!

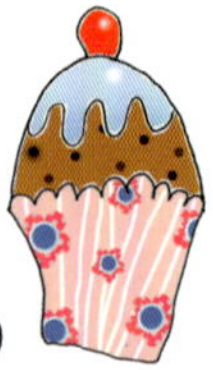

The Christmas holidays wouldn't be complete without a special outing to Bath's beautiful Theatre Royal to see the pantomime, with Bonne Bonne. Rosie and Flo laugh as the pantomime dame sings silly songs and their friends from the dancing school perform on stage. Flo looks forward to the moment when Bonne Bonne asks ...'Who'd like an ice cream?!'

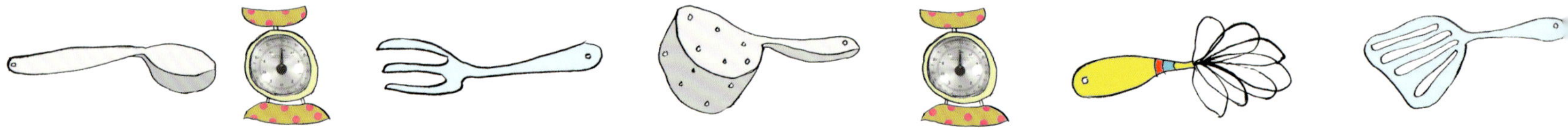

Easy Chocolate Ice Cream

300ml (1/2 pint) double cream
200gm tinned condensed milk (half a small tin) (7oz)
50gm (2oz) cocoa powder
100gm (4oz) chopped chocolate (milk, plain, white or mixed)

Whisk the first three ingredients together to form a thick airy mixture.
Gently stir in the chopped chocolate.
Tip the mixture into a small ice cream container with lid.
Freeze for about 6 hours or overnight.
Serve straight from the freezer with wafers, or in a cone.

This is Flo's favourite flavour!

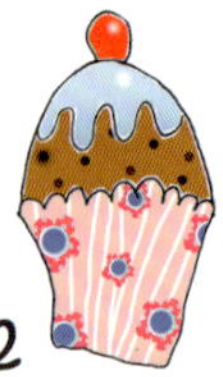

Recipe Index

Recipe Index

Recipe Index

Baking notes

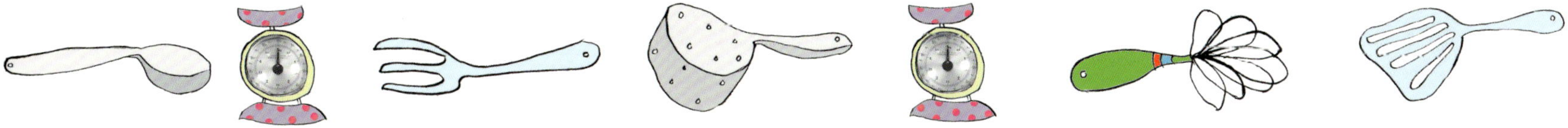

Baking notes

About the author & illustrator

Amanda Overeynder was born, and has lived most of her life, in the beautiful city of Bath. She started cooking at a young age, following in the footsteps of her mother, Bonne Bonne, who trained in Home Economics as a contemporary of Mary Berry, at Bath College. Amanda qualified as a dietician and worked as a hospital dietician within the NHS for several years, lecturing in Food and Nutrition too, before settlin to a rewarding career as a primary school teacher, at Monkton Combe School, Bath. Amanda is married and has two daughters, who share her love of cooking. Amanda is passionate about the role of food and eating as a sociable event which brings people together, encouraging friendshi and communication, whilst establishing good habits for a healthy lifestyle.

Susie Grindey was born in North Wales. She lived there until she went to university in 1993 to study Animation and Graphics. After graduating she lived in Penarth and worked as a graphic designer in Cardiff. After working for 4 years as a designer she gradually moved into painting which is her big love and in 2001 became a full-time painter. She has a particular love of Welsh coastlines and quirky architectural features. She loves bright colours, textures, typography, fabrics, old bits of paper and anything that sparkles!; these all feature in her paintings. On every piece of work she likes to sew a heart as she only paints places she really loves. Susie hopes her paintings are cheerful and make people smile when they see them! Susie is married with two children and lives in the Wye Valley.